Ulrich Renz / Barbara Brinkmann

Somn uşor, micule lup

Dormi bene, piccolo lupo

O carte cu ilustraţii în două limbi

Traducere:

Stefan Gitman, Prague, Czech Republic (română)

Margherita Haase, Lübeck, Germany (italiană)

sefa

Little Wolf would like to meet you at his home:

www.childrens-books-bilingual.com

"Noapte bună, Tim! Vom continua să căutăm mâine.
Somn uşor!"

"Buona notte, Tim! Domani continuiamo a cercare.
Adesso però dormi bene!"

Afară este deja întuneric.

Fuori è già buio.

Ce face Tim acolo?

Ma cosa fa Tim?

Iese afară, se duce la locul de joacă.

Pe cine caută oare acolo?

Va al parco giochi.

Che cosa sta cercando?

Pe micul lup!

Nu poate dormi fără el.

Il piccolo lupo.

Senza di lui non riesce a dormire.

Cine vine acum?

Ma chi sta arrivando?

Marie!
Ea îşi caută mingea.

Marie!
Lei sta cercando la sua palla.

Şi oare ce caută Tobi?

E Tobi cosa cerca?

Excavatorul lui.

La sua ruspa.

Şi oare ce caută Nala?

E cosa cerca Nala?

Păpuşa ei.

La sua bambola.

Copiii ăştia nu trebuie să se ducă la culcare?
Pisica se miră.

Ma i bambini non devono andare a letto?
Il gatto si meraviglia.

Cine vine acum?

E adesso chi sta arrivando?

Mama şi tatăl lui Tim!

Ei nu pot dormi fără Tim.

La mamma e il papà di Tim.

Senza il loro Tim non riescono a dormire.

Şi acum vin mai mulţi! Tatăl Mariei.

Bunicul lui Tobi. Şi mama Nalei.

Ed ecco che arrivano anche altri!

Il papà di Marie. Il nonno di Tobi. E la mamma di Nala.

Acum repede în pătuţ!

Ma adesso svelti a letto!

"Noapte bună, Tim.
Nu mai e nevoie să căutăm mâine."

"Buona notte, Tim!
Domani non dobbiamo più cercare."

"Somn uşor, micule lup!"

"Dormi bene, piccolo lupo!"

More about me ...

Children's Books for the Global Village

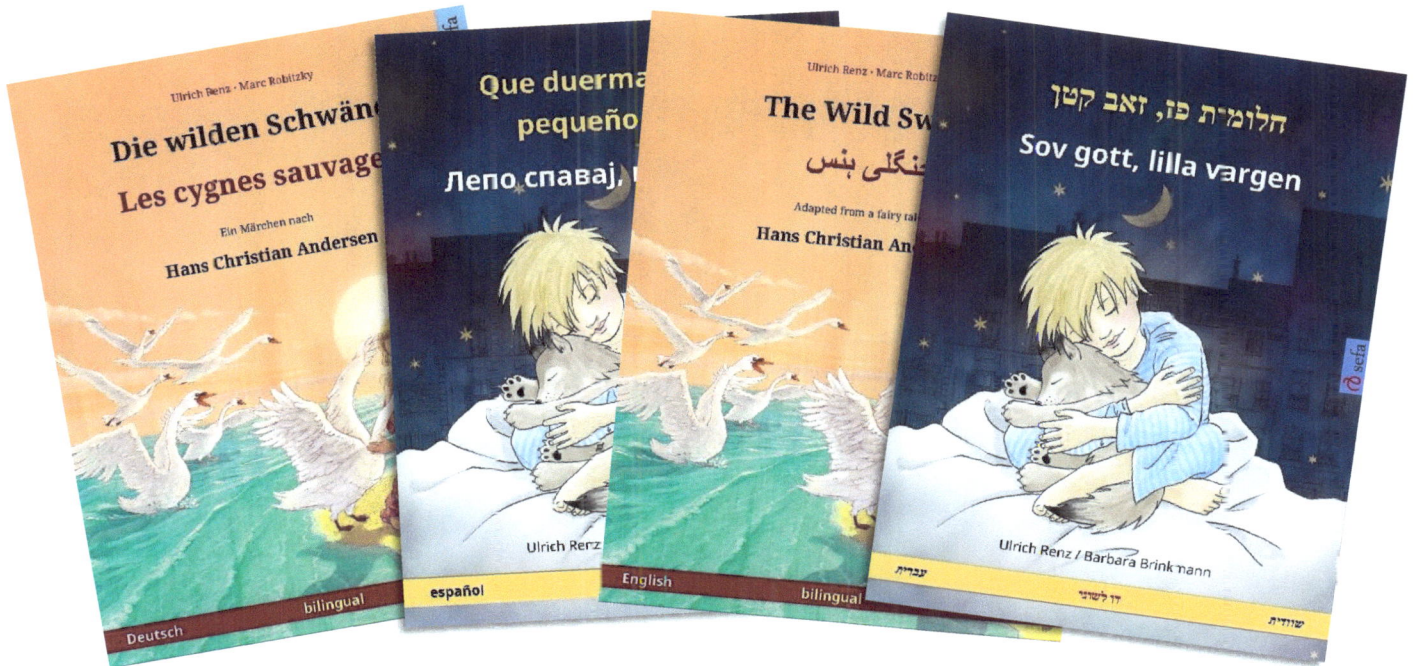

Ulrich Renz · Marc Robitzky

Die wilden Schwän...
Les cygnes sauvage...

Ein Märchen nach
Hans Christian Andersen

Deutsch — bilingual

Que duerma...
pequeño...
Лепо спавај, ...

español — bilingual

Ulrich Renz...

The Wild Sw...
...نگلی هنس

Adapted from a fairy tal...
Hans Christian An...

English — bilingual

חלומית פז, זאב קטן
Sov gott, lilla vargen

Ulrich Renz / Barbara Brinkmann

עברית — דו לשוני — שוודית

Ever more children are born away from their parents' home countries, and are balancing between the languages of their mother, their father. their grandparents, and their peers. Our bilingual books are meant to help bridge the language divides that cross more and more families, neighborhoods and kindergartens in the globalized world.

Little Wolf also proposes:

The Wild Swans

Bilingual picture book
adapted from
a fairy tale by
Hans Christian Andersen

▶ Reading age 4 and up

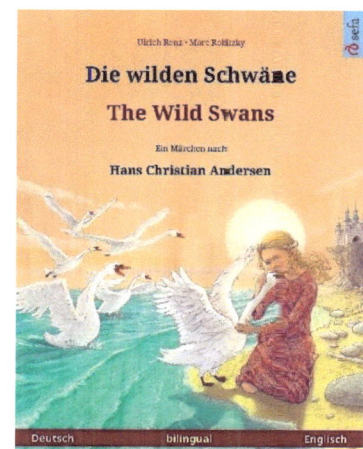

Ulrich Renz · Marc Robitzky

Die wilden Schwäne
The Wild Swans

Ein Märchen nach
Hans Christian Andersen

Deutsch — bilingual — Englisch

www.childrens-books-bilingual.com

NEW! Little Wolf in Sign Language

Home	Authors	Little Wolf	About

Bilingual Children's Books - in any language you want

Welcome to Little Wolf's Language Wizard!

Just choose the two languages in which you want to read to your children:

Language 1:

French

Language 2:

Icelandic

Go!

Learn more about our bilingual books at www.childrens-books-bilingual.com. At the heart of this website you will find what we call our "Language Wizard". It contains more than 60 languages and any of their bilingual combinations: Just select, in a simple drop-down-menu, the two languages in which you'd like to read "Little Wolf" or "The Wild Swans" to your child – and the book is instantly made available, ready for order as an ebook download or as a printed edition.

As time goes by ...

... the little ones grow older, and start to read on their own. Here is Little Wolf's recommendation to them:

Smart detective stories for smart children

Reading age: 10 + - www.bo-and-friends.com

Wie die Zeit vergeht ...

Irgendwann sind aus den süßen Kleinen süße Große geworden

– die jetzt sogar selber lesen können. Der kleine Wolf empfiehlt:

Kinderkrimis zum Mitdenken

Lesealter ab 10 – www.motte-und-co.de

About the authors

Ulrich Renz was born in Stuttgart, Germany, in 1960. After studying French literature in Paris he graduated from medical school in Lübeck and worked as head of a scientific publishing company. He is now a writer of non-fiction books as well as children's fiction books. – www.ulrichrenz.de

Barbara Brinkmann was born in Munich, Germany, in 1969. She grew up in the foothills of the Alps and studied architecture and medicine for a while in Munich. She now works as a freelance graphic artist, illustrator and writer. – www.bcbrinkmann.com

© 2017 by Sefa Verlag Kirsten Bödeker, Lübeck, Germany
www.sefa-verlag.de

sefa

Database: Paul Bödeker, München, Germany
Font: Noto Sans

ISBN: 9783739904382

Version: 20170513